(un)Fashion by Tibor + Maira Kalman.   Booth-Clibborn Editions

(un)FASHION

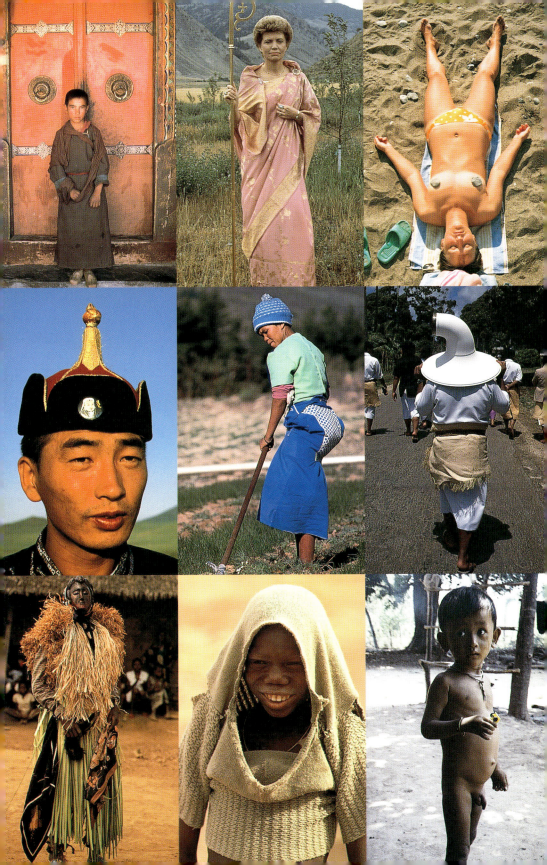

BODY ART

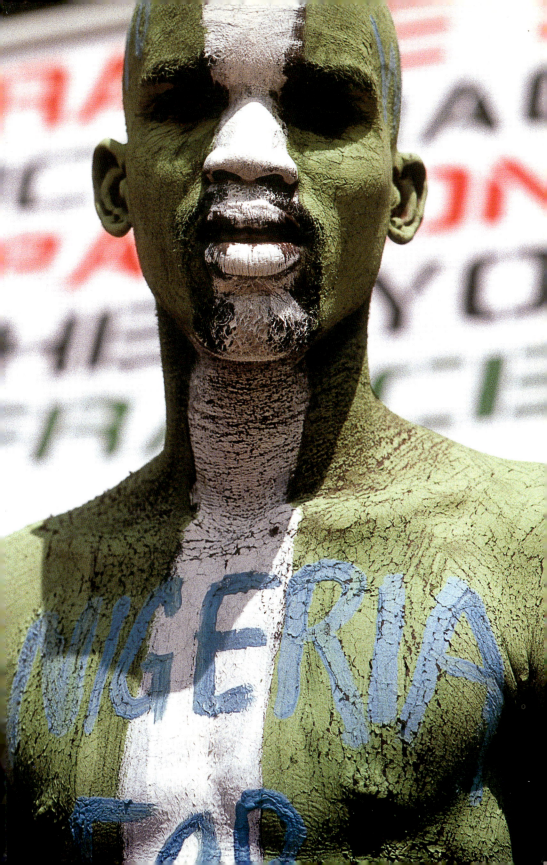

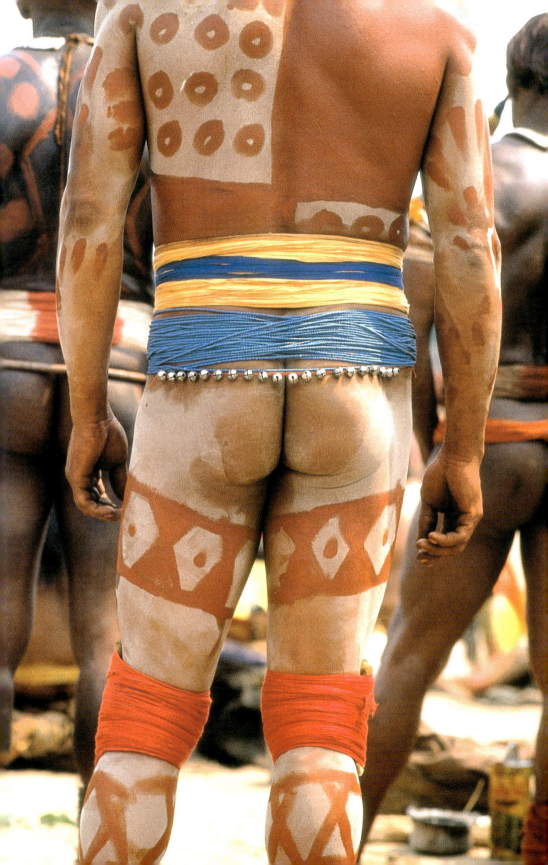

ACCESSORIES

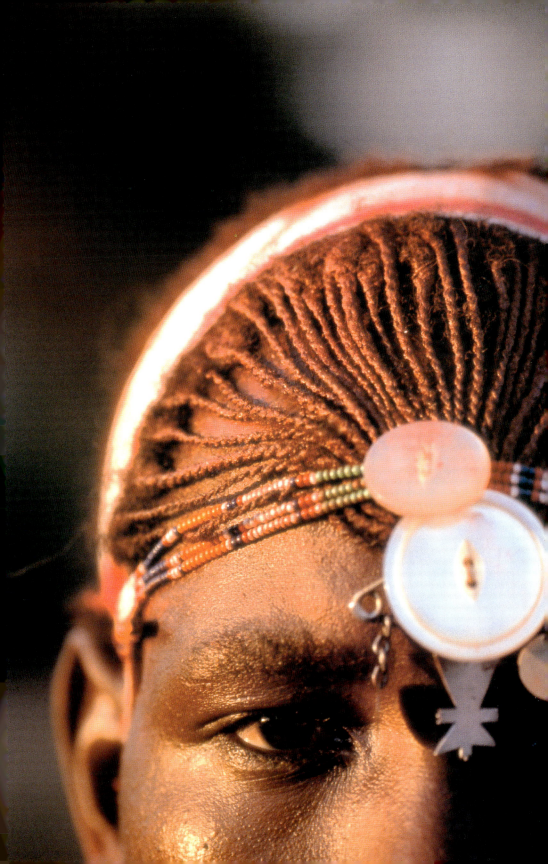

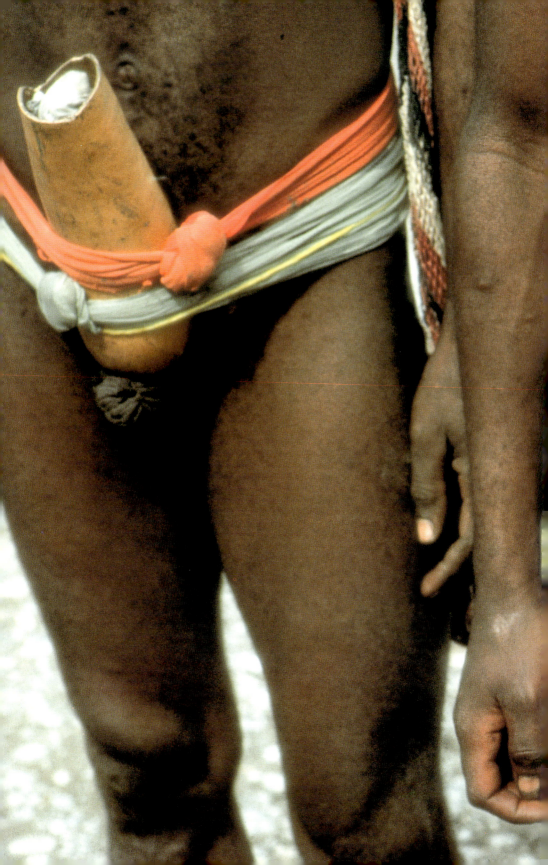

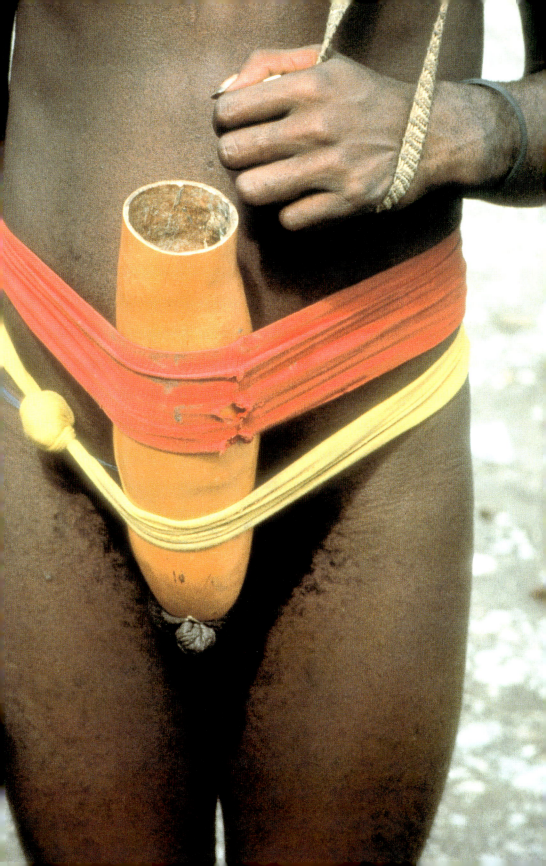

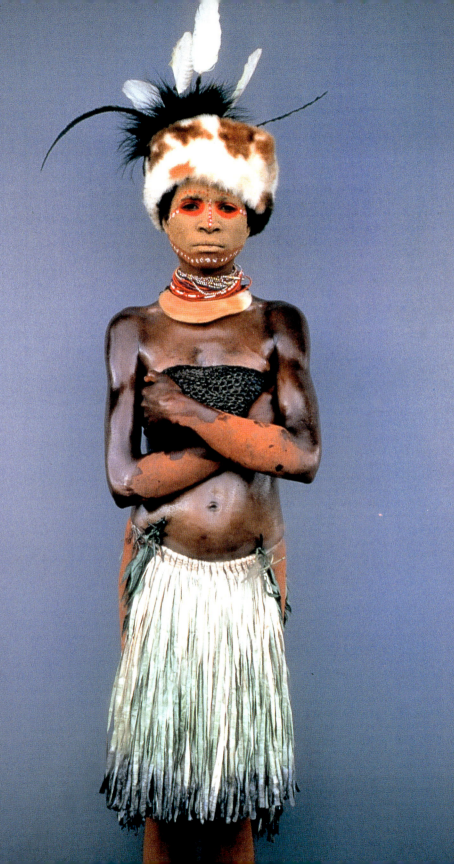

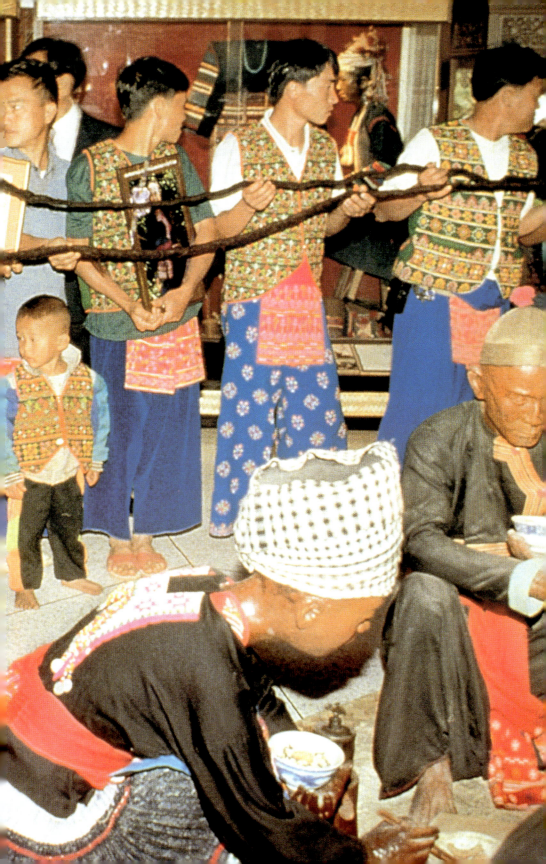

OPTICS

DRESSED TO KILL

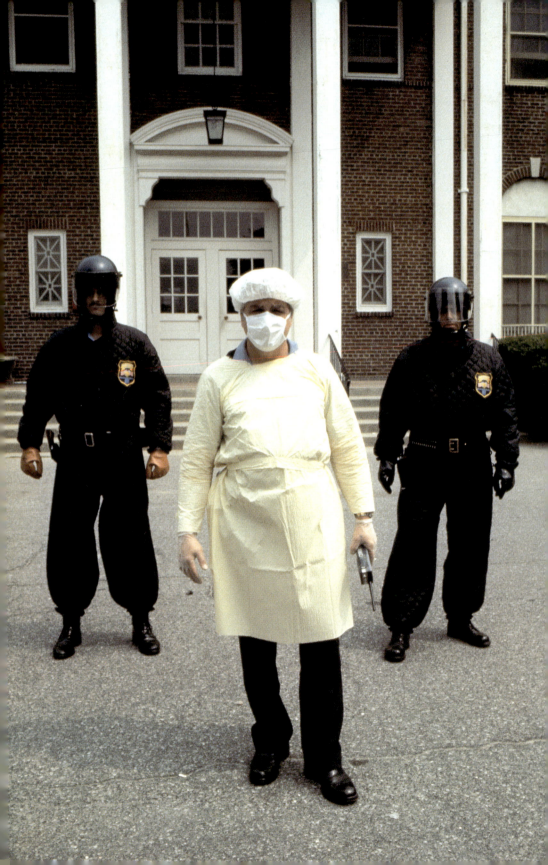

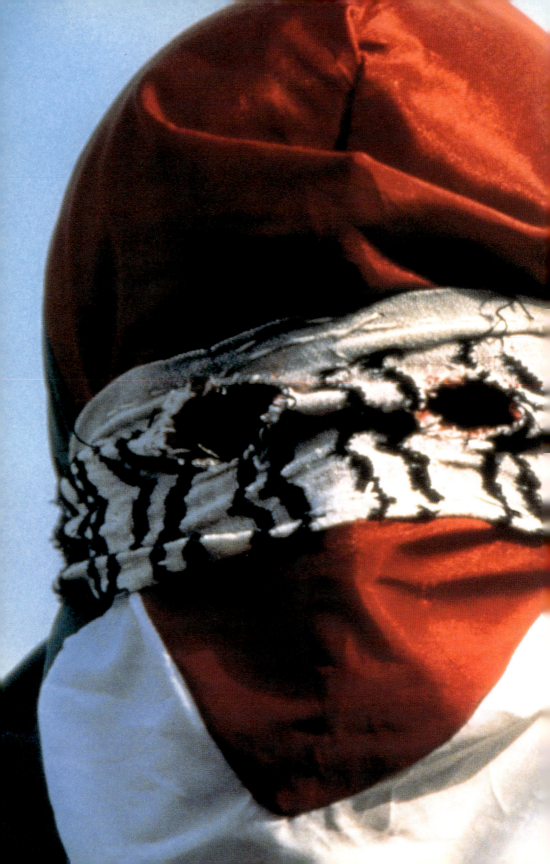

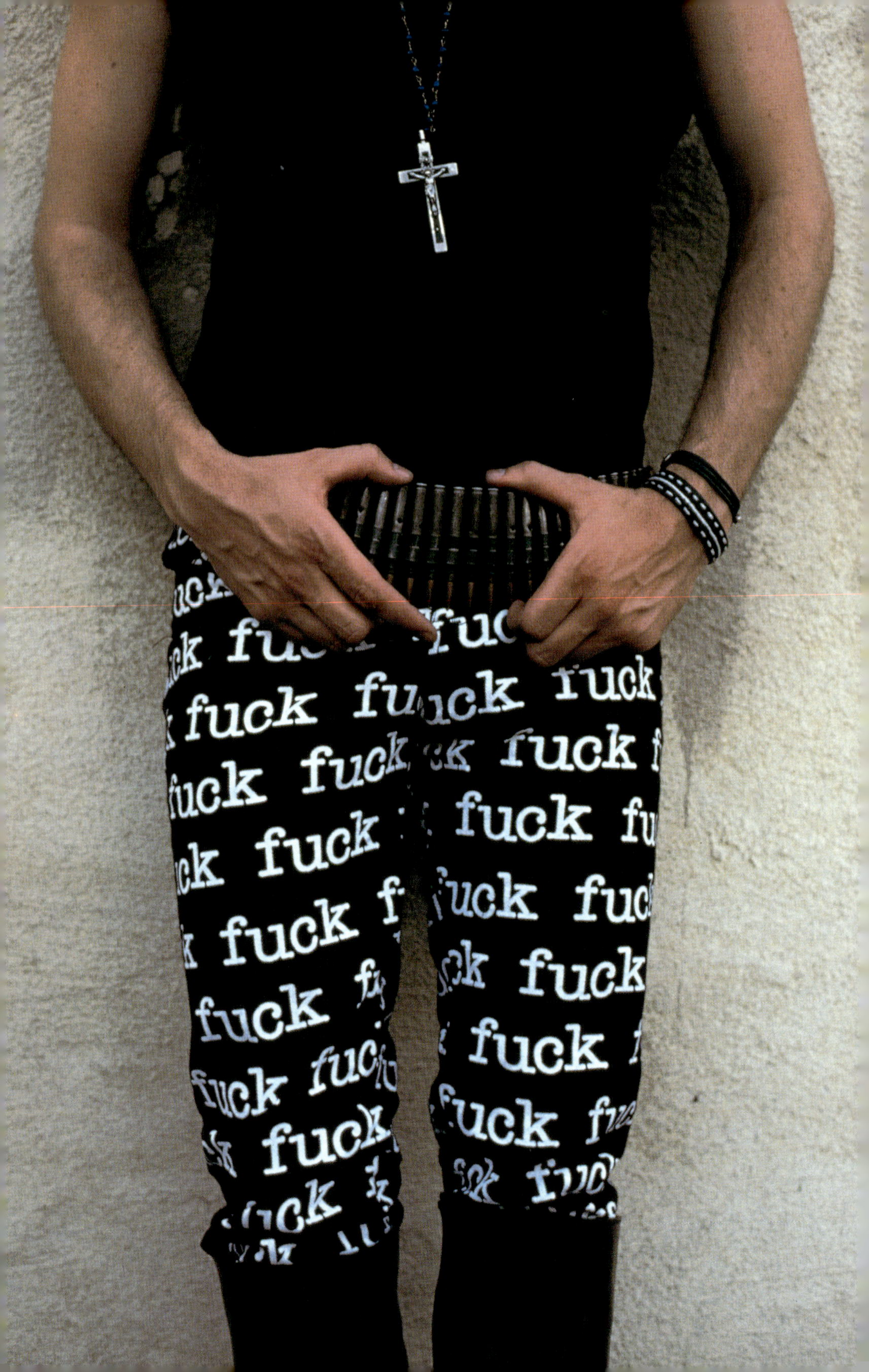

MASKS

(un)MENTIONABLES

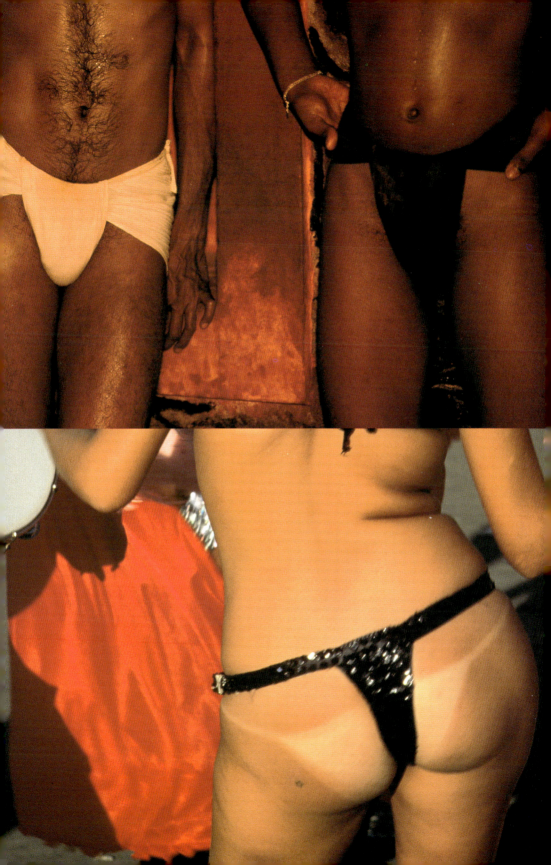

MODESTY

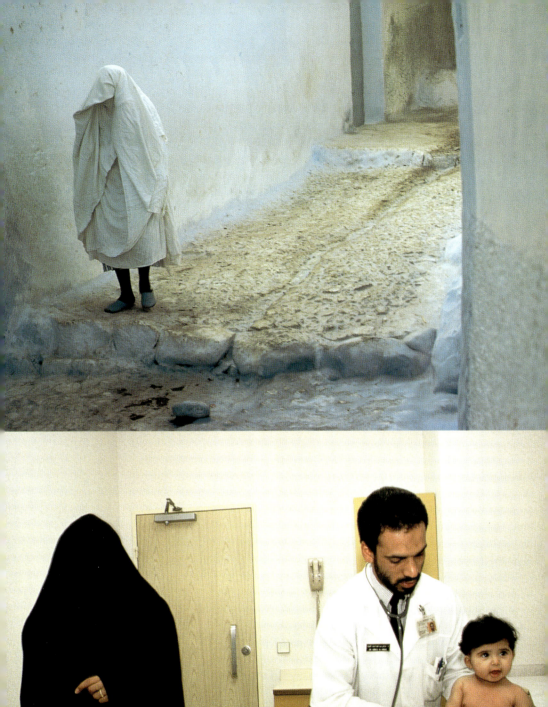
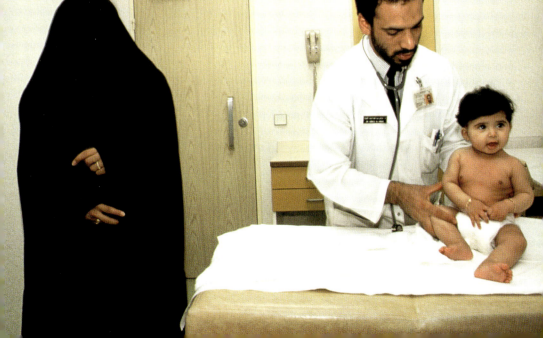

MOBILE HOME

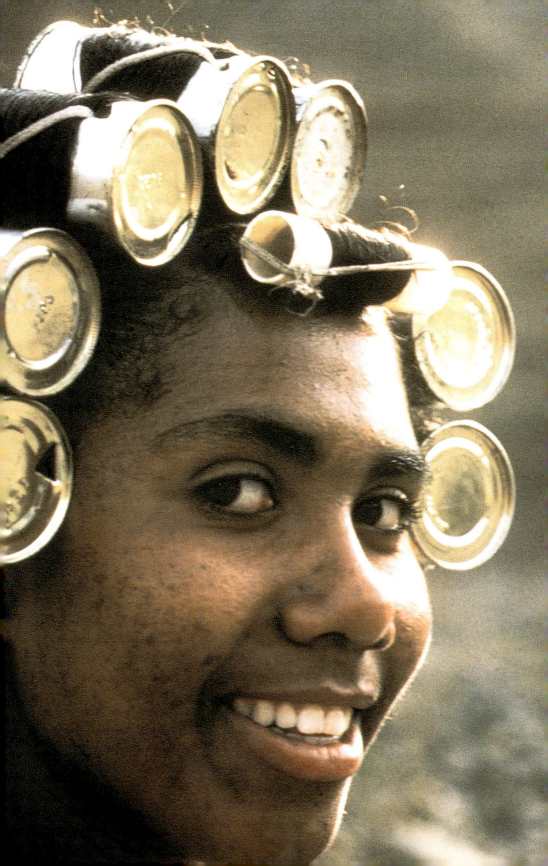

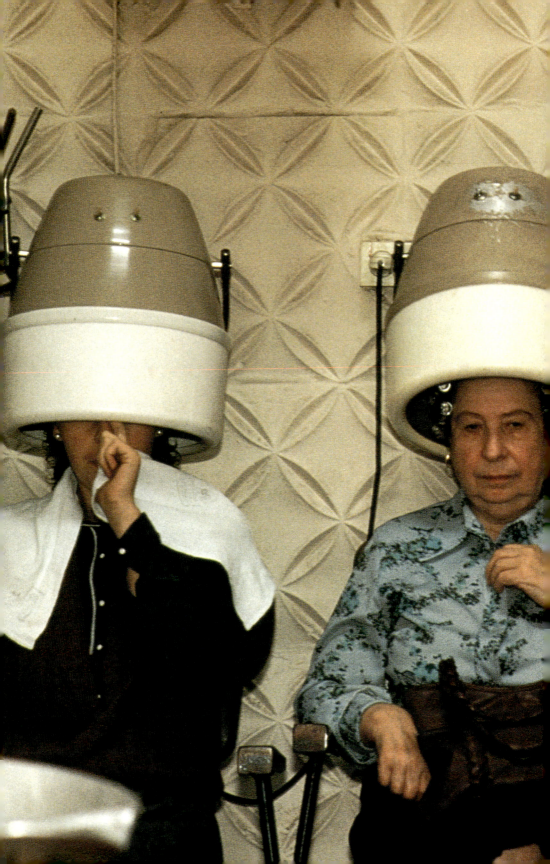

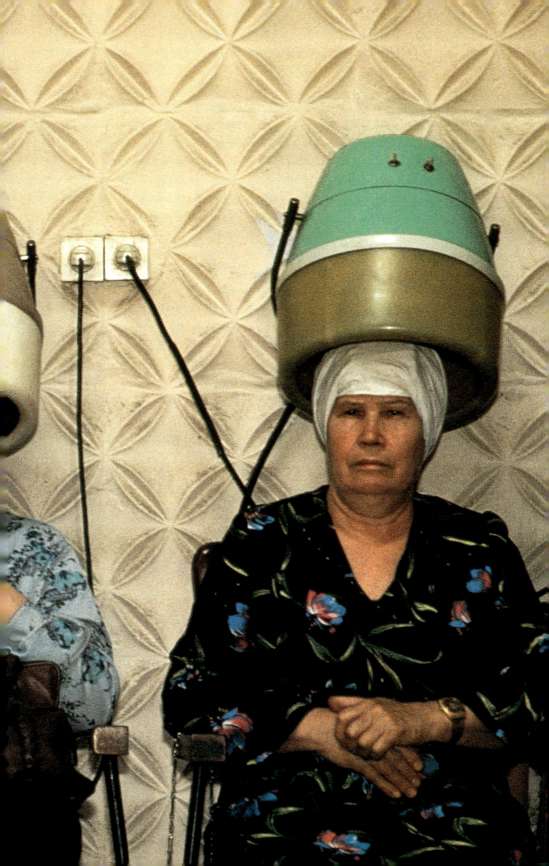

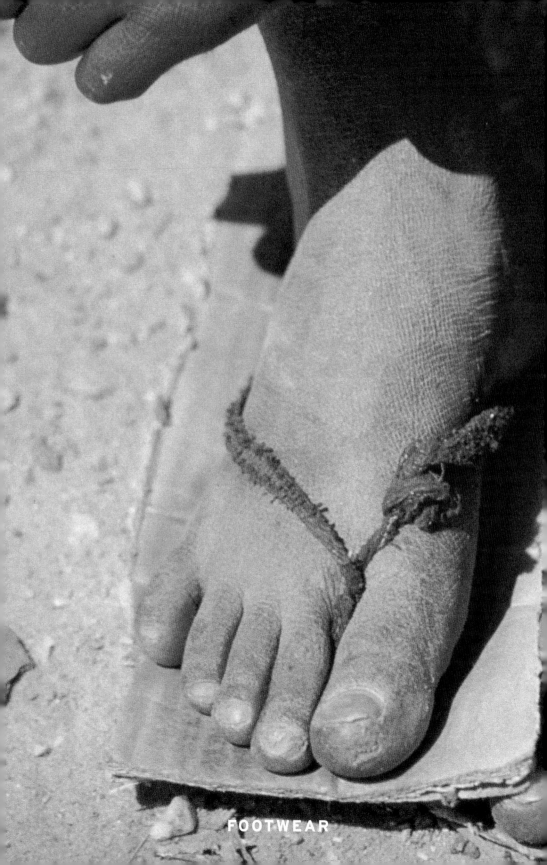

FOOTWEAR

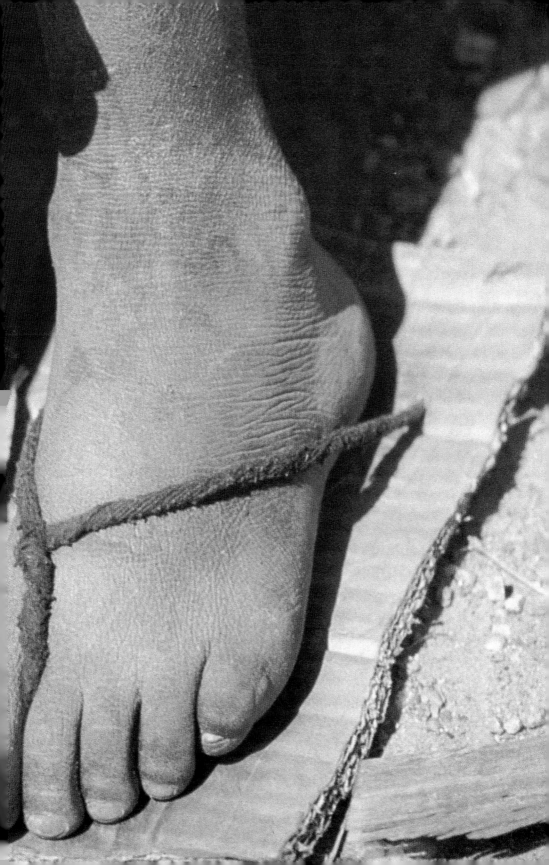

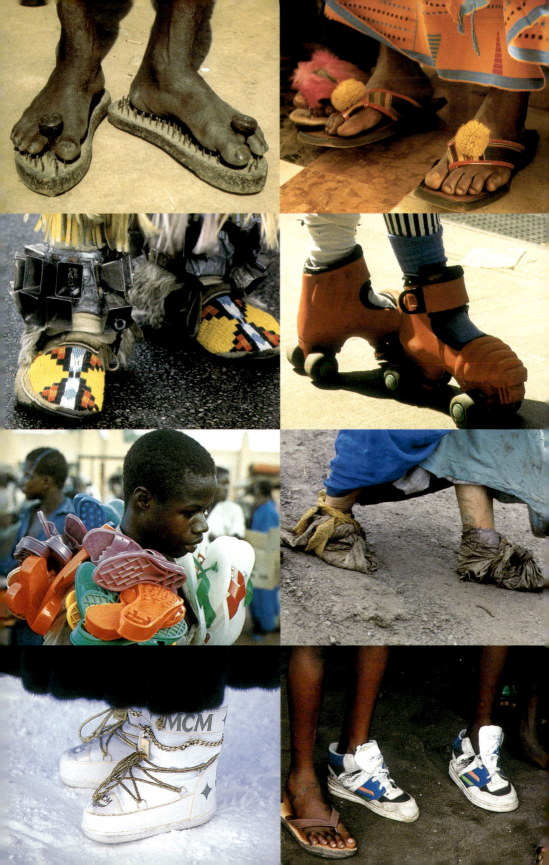

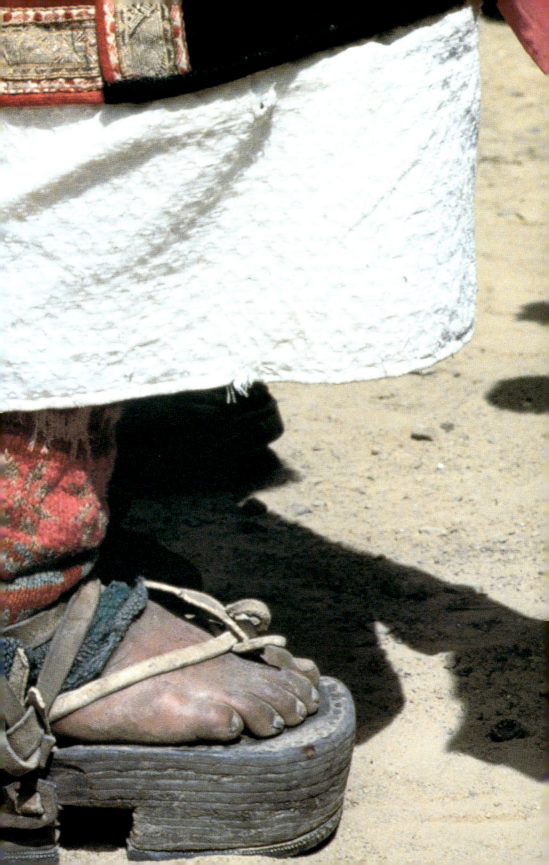

HUMAN STORE

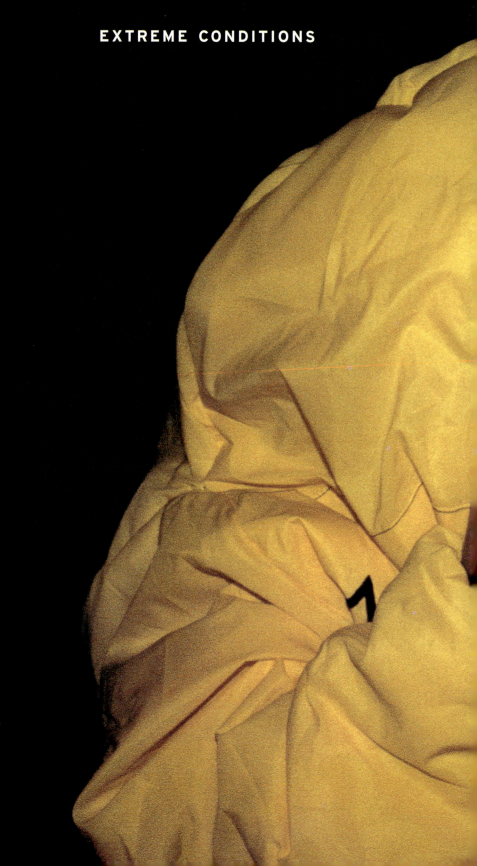

VERY EXTREME CONDITIONS

SOLOS

DUOS

HOLY WEAR

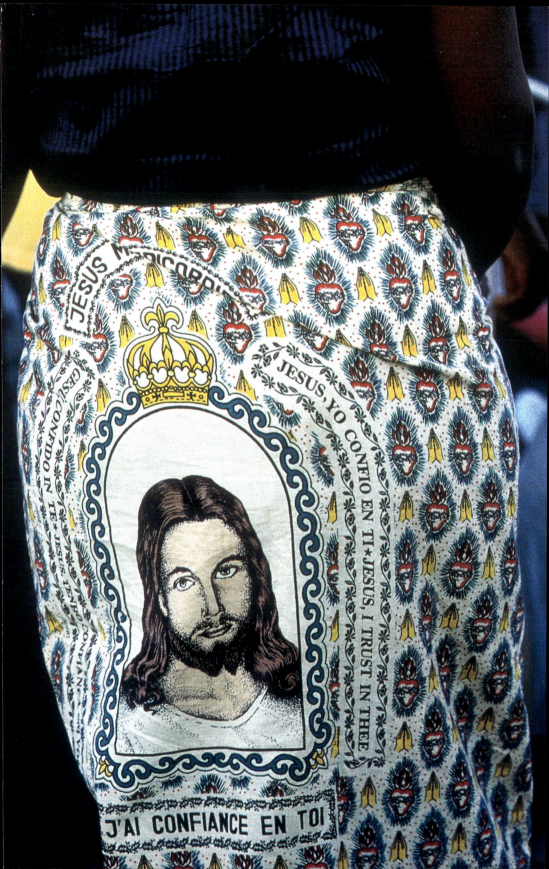

DEATH

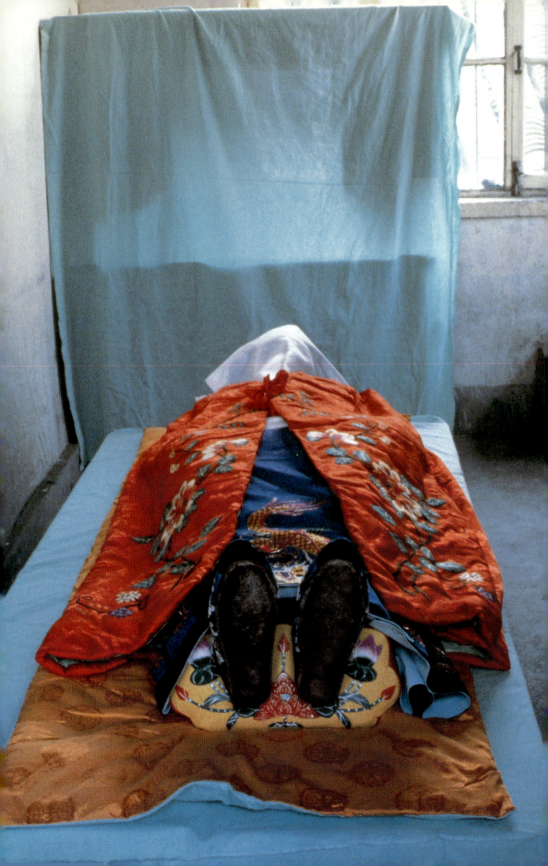

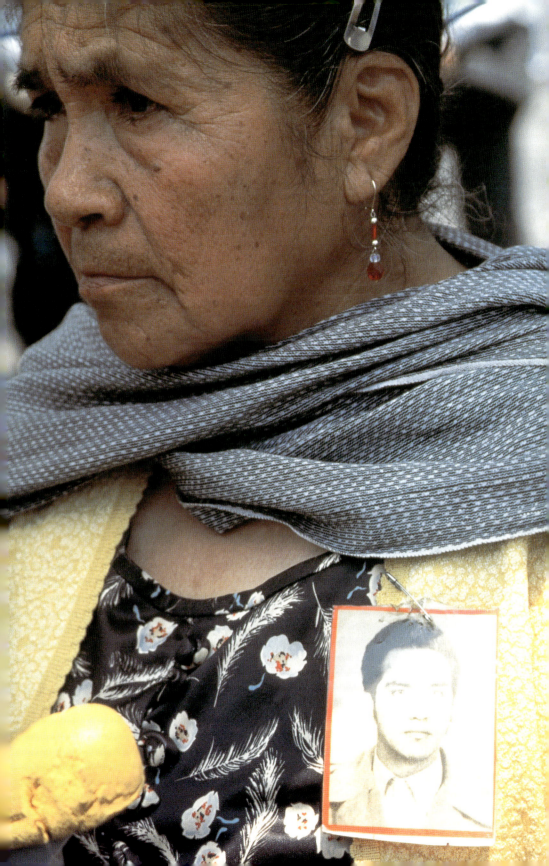

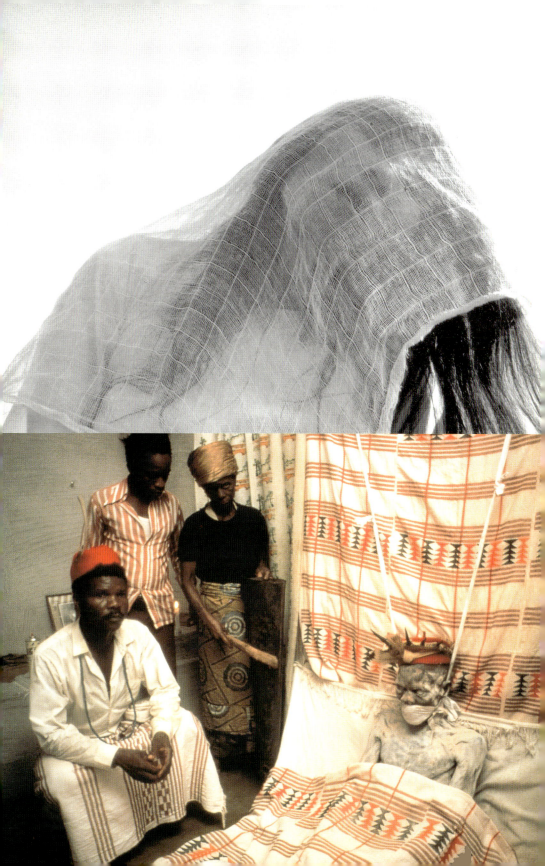

(re)BIRTH

In our daily travels Tibor
and I were always looking
for insane, inspired and
beautiful stuff. There were
no limits—high art, low art,
minimalism, maximalism,
ad hocism, garbage—it was
all fascinating and important
to us. This book was initiated
by Tibor a few years before
he died. He happily dove
(fully dressed) into an ocean
of images and ideas. In his
Tiborian way, he wanted to
catalog his giddy obsession
with mankind's ingenious
expression. All of the photo-
graphs are current. We are
not digging up nostalgia. We
salute the present and the
future of the indomitable
human spirit.

And, I might add,
this book is for
Tibor.

Maira Kalman

COVER

Family in Gobi desert,
Mongolia
*Gueorgui Pinkhassov/
Magnum*

(un)Fashion

Fig leaf, Garden of Eden
Chalkie Davies

Elvis impersonator, USA
Sydney Byrd/Liaison Agency

Two men carrying
umbrellas, Mali
Ian Berry/Magnum

Woman with red flag,
Mongolia, China
Eve Arnold/Magnum

Man with snake, USA
Steve McCurry/Magnum

Military cadets, Philippines
Steve McCurry/Magnum

Two hip cats, Japan
Bruno Barbey/Magnum

Huli wig man painting face,
Papua New Guinea
Wendy Stone/Liaison Agency

Man with red scarf, Namibia
Alon Reininger/Contact Press

Woman with pot on head
Christiana Dittman

Tribesman wearing penis
sheath. Bigger the
sheath, higher the rank,
Papua New Guinea
Haglund-Unep/Still Pictures

Charles Manson dress, USA
Paul Souders/Liaison Agency

Dapper man in red hat,
South Africa
Alon Reininger/Contact Press

Man dressed for funeral of
Diana, Princess of Wales, UK
Bruno Barbey/Magnum

Three men with canes,
Namibia
Alon Reininger/Contact Press

Woman with red umbrella,
Tonga
Dilip Mehta/Contact Press

Orthodox Jew, Israel
Daniel Laine/Liaison Agency

Seated tribal chief,
Ivory Coast
*M & E Bernheim/
Woodfin Camp*

Man with turban, Africa
David Burnett/Contact Press

Three people, South Africa
Alon Reininger/Contact Press

The Burryman, thistle man
representing ancient fertility
god, Scotland
Homer Sykes/Woodfin Camp

Gay march, USA
Everke/Liaison Agency

Sandwich boy, USA
Maira Kalman

Skater kid, USA
Charles Thompson

Girlie tee shirt, Colombia
Gilles Peress/Magnum

Boy in front of orange
doors, India
*Roland & Sabrina Michaud/
Woodfin Camp*

Leader of Universal
& Triumphant Church,
Montana, USA
Akhtar Hussein/Sygma

Sunbather at Yalta
beach, Ukraine
Martin Parr/Magnum

Man in hat worn to connect
person with heaven, Mongolia
Thierry Falise/Liaison Agency

Woman farming, South Africa
Alon Reininger/Contact Press

Woman with headpiece,
Tonga
Dilip Mehta/Contact Press

Man in Ekpe Secret Society
costume, Cameroon
Edward Parker/Still Pictures

Boy wearing sweater over
head, Burkina Faso
Paul Harrison/Still Pictures

Naked boy, Cambodia
Meaghan Kombol

BODY ART

Sadhu Holi Festival, India
Lindsay Hebberd/
Woodfin Camp

Tribesman with painted face,
Papua New Guinea
Eric Meola/Image Bank

Tattooed Maori, New Zealand
Art Wolfe

Man with painted white
stripe, Papua New Guinea
Art Wolfe

Pushkar festival, India
Mark Graham/Liaison Agency

Soccer supporter, Nigeria
Chris Steele-Perkins/Magnum

Shaman festival, China
Xue Yan

Spotted man with goggle
mask, Indonesia
Kal Muller/Woodfin Camp

Kewa woman in mourning,
Papua New Guinea
P. J. Griffiths/Magnum

Woman with painted
white face, Barranquilla
Carnival, Columbia
Jeremy Hormer/
Liaison Agency

Mud Man, New Guinea—
Mourners cover themselves
with thick layers of clay.
When clay falls off,
the mourning is over
Malcom S. Kirk/Peter Arnold

Painted back of Xingu
Indian, Brazil
Ricardo Beliel/Liaison Agency

ACCESSORIES

Masai wearing pineapple
can earring, Kenya
Pete Turner/Image Bank

Wedding headdress, India
Lindsay Hebberd/
Woodfin Camp

Woman wearing vest
with buttons, USA
Peter Essick/Aurora

Woman with jewelry, India
Lindsay Hebberd/
Woodfin Camp

Highlander tribesman
wearing yogurt lid through
his nose, Papua New Guinea
P. J. Griffiths/Magnum

Woman with pearl necklace
at polo match, UK
Martin Parr/Magnum

Condom necklace, USA
Thomas Hoepker/Magnum

Long Cou woman, with neck
rings worn to enhance their
beauty. Women begin adding
30 pound rings to their necks
at the age of 5, Burma
J. Witt/Sipa

Saddam Hussein watch, Iraq
Steve McCurry/Magnum

Mackeral can bracelet,
Papua New Guinea
P.J. Griffiths/Magnum

The Apatani women are
considered so beautiful that
their husbands plug their
noses with bamboo strips
to prevent them from being
kidnapped by neighboring
tribesman, India
Lindsay Hebberd/
Woodfin Camp

Masai tribesman with button
headpiece, Kenya
Eric Meola/Image Bank

Asmat tribesmen with penis
gourds, Indonesia
Bruno Barbey/Magnum

TRIBES

Hulie Girl, New Guinea
Malcom S. Kirk/Peter Arnold

Man wearing poncho,
Ecuador
Desjardins—Tapador/Sipa

Voodoo man with staff,
Jamaica
Dennis Stock/Magnum

2000 Zulu virgins take
part in annual spring rite,
South Africa
Tim Zielenbach/
Contact Press

Standing couple, South Africa
Alon Reininger/Contact Press

Kayapo Indians in costume
for the Bemo Festival, Brazil
Miguel Rio Branco/Magnum

Newlyweds, Mongolia
Michel Setboun/Sygma

Tarahumara Indians, Mexico
Kal Muller/Woodfin Camp

Young horsemen, Mongolia
Patricio Estay/Liaison Agency

Hasidic man and children
Daniel Laine

Sorcerer Hu Sengla's 17-foot-
long locks of hair, Thailand
Bano/Sipa

Tribesmen dancing, Kenya
Christopher Arnesen/
Tony Stone

The son of the Emir of
Kano, Nigeria
Bruno Barbey/Magnum

STANDARD ISSUE

Schoolboy, Cuba
Angelo Cavalli/Sipa

Police motorcycle race, Japan
J.P. Laffont/Sygma

Traffic cop, Ghana
Stuart Franklin/Sygma

Women at National Day
March, Malaysia
Abbas/Magnum

Futuristic costumes on
National Day, Malaysia
Stuart Franklin/Magnum

Lifeguards, Australia
Klaus Bossemeyer/Aurora

Military police, Fiji
Steven Burr Williams/
Liaison Agency

School of Bullfighting,
Arles, France
Jose Nicolas/Liaison Agency

Children at carnival, Belgium
Frilet/Sipa

Three women in red, Namibia
Alon Reininger/Contact

Dallas Cowboy cheerleaders.
Each applicant is judged on
her: Enthusiasm, Poise,
Showmanship, Dance, Tech-
nique, Personal Appearance
Figure, Personality, Energy,
High Kicks, and Splits, USA
George Rose/Liaison Agency

Nanny School, UK
Armineh Johannes/Sipa

WWII veterans dancing,
Russia
Fridrikh Grinberg

OPTICS

Man with red sunglasses at
Doo-Dah parade, USA
Peter Essick/Aurora

Man with glasses held
by string, India
J. & D. Duooin/Sygma

Woman sunbathing, Spain
Martin Parr/Magnum

Man wearing ski goggles,
Afghanistan
Abbas/Magnum

Virtual Reality Glasses at
an Allman Brothers Show
Woodstock, 1994, USA
Bob Strong/Sipa

Men in white, Niger
Chris Brown/Saba

Boy wearing makeshift
glasses, Indonesia
Tara Sosrowardoya/
Liaison Agency

Woman in chador, Kuwait
Abbas/Magnum

DRESSED TO KILL

Sandinista rebel, Nicaragua
Alon Reininger/Contact Press

Prison guards in protective
suits, USA
Owen Franken/Sygma

Naval training, China
Chine Nouvelle/Sipa

Army recruits in camouflage,
Philippines
Susan Meiselas/Magnum

FBI SWAT team, USA
Remi Benali/Liaison Agency

Costumes for Chinese New
Year festival, Singapore
Jim Anderson/Woodfin Camp

Man with axe, Israel
Photographer unknown

Liberian guerilla with
pocketbook
Patrick Robert/Sygma

Man in loincloth, Afghanistan
Alfred/Sipa

Fuck pants, USA
Steve McCurry/Magnum

Teenage member of the
Circle Piru Bloods, USA
Jim Tynan/Impact Visuals

Women in military parade,
Afghanistan
Abbas/Magnum

Children in military
training, China
Thomas/Sygma

Police woman in civilian
clothes, France
Patrick Zachmann/Magnum

Well-armed 105-year-old
woman, Armenia
Johannes/Sipa

Young boy with rifle, Brazil
Miguel Rio Branco/Magnum

FACEMASKS

Traditional Indian rebel
mask, Nicaragua
Susan Meiselas/Magnum

Protective mask, Indonesia
V. Miladinovic/Sygma

Man and boy wear anti-
pollution masks, China
Steve McCurry/Magnum

Pilgrim in Qoyllur ritual, Peru
E. Pasquier/Sygma

Woman sunbathing, UK
Martin Parr/Magnum

Three boys in water, who are
using the cloth to protect their
face from being stung by poi-
sonous jellyfish, Philippines
*Michael Friedel/
Woodfin Camp*

Archers, Japan
Patricio Estoy/Liaison Agency

School child, Indonesia
Paul Lowe/Magnum

Red Army dog in gas
mask, Russia
Tass/Sovfoto/Eastfoto

Basque festival, Basques,
Spain
Joanna P. Pinneo, Aurora

(un)MENTIONABLES

Statue, Chinatown, NY
Eve Arnold/Magnum

Selling women's bustiers,
Cuba
Bob Strong/Sipa

Farmer plowing, Sri Lanka
David Burnett/Contact Press

Woman wearing underpants
in the street, USA
Tony Savino/Sipa

1995 French Open, France
Art Seitz/Liaison Agency

Kalarippayat martial arts
loincloths, India
Remy Benali/Liaison Agency

Street dancer shaking her
booty during Carnival, Brazil
Miguel Rio Branco/Magnum

Bathers, Nepal
Dilip Mehta/Contact Press

MODESTY

Breasts bursting out
of bra, USA
Peter Martens/Magnum

Cloaked and hooded figures
with sticks, South Africa
Alon Reininger/Contact Press

Two Uygur women,
Kashgar, China
Abbas/Magnum

Shrouded figure in
passageway, Morocco
Harry Gruyaert/Magnum

Veiled mother watches baby
being treated, Saudi Arabia
Abbas/Magnum

Masked woman, Oman
*Christian Vioujard/
Liaison Agency*

Veiled woman,
United Arab Emirates
Eve Arnold/Magnum

Hippie in front of his van,
Goa, India
George Shelley

Woman at school, Sudan
Abbas/Magnum

MOBILE HOME

Seated woman with
baby, Nigeria
Bruno Barbey/Magnum

Man with great-grandson,
India
J & D Ducoin/Sygma

Woman with leather baby
carrier, Namibia
Alon Reininger/Contact Press

Inuit girl and child, Canada
*Eastcott/Momatiuk/
Woodfin Camp*

Women in Turquoise, Mali
Abbas/Magnum

Children, Afghanistan
Reza/Liaison Agency

Girl with baby, Nepal
Marc Riboud/Magnum

Native American baby
in bundle, USA
David Alan Harvey/Magnum

Black woman with white
child, South Africa
Alon Reininger/Contact Press

Woman in black with baby,
Mauritania
J. P. Laffont/Sygma

Yanomami Indian mother
taking picture, Brazil
Nick Nichols/Magnum

Miao woman and child,
Southwestern China
*Rapahel Gaillarde/
Liaison Agency*

Two children carrying
infants, Guatemala
Thomas Hoepker/Magnum

HEADGEAR

Man in prayer. His head-
dress represents his
aspiration towards heaven,
Dharamsula, India
Raghu Rai/Magnum

Basket hats, India
Bruno Barbey/Magnum

Refugees with red cups,
Rwanda
*Jean-Claude Coutausse/
Contact Press*

Man with floral headdress,
Papua New Guinea
W. Stone/Liaison Agency

Two men in bowler hats, UK
Armineh/Sipa Press

Crowd at Festival of San
Marcial, Spain
Joanna B. Pinneo/Aurora

People with Red Cross
hats, Spain
Dilip Mehta/Contact Press

Women with straw hats,
Jamaica
Dennis Stock/Magnum

Mourning hat
*Jean-Michel Joge/
Figaro Magazine*

Iman tribal man with
medals, Malaysia
Michael S. Yamashita

Woman with tin can rollers,
Cape Verde
Michael Friedel

Three ladies under
hairdryers, Ukraine
Bruno Barbey/Magnum

Woman with pen clipped to
headband, South Africa
Alon Reininger/Contact Press

T'Boli woman in costume, Catobato, Phillipines
Bruno Barbey/Magnum

Newspaper hats on campus Berkeley, CA
Paul Fusco/Magnum

Zulu dancer, South Africa
Alon Reininger/Contact Press

Tuareg girl with hair tuft, Mali
Steve McCurry/Magnum

Football fanatic, USA
George Rose/Liaison Agency

Man with hat and flower, Haiti
Thomas Hoepker/Magnum

Refugee with container on head, Sudan
Jean-Claude Coutasse/ Contact Press

Woman wearing Jalbab (full-body shroud) with bird on her head, Afghanistan
Thomas Abercrombie/ National Geographic

Man in high turban, India
Dilip Mehta/Contact Press

High-ranking military man in ceremonial headdress, India
Lindsay Hebberd/ Woodfin Camp

FOOTWEAR

Cardboard sandals, Mozambique
Guenay Ulutuncok/Laif

Military recruits, China
Chine Nouvelle/Sipa

Women shopping for shoes, Afghanistan
Steve McCurry/Magnum

Three villagers' feet, Faryab Province
Reza/Liaison Agency

Women in black robes and white pumps with black and white sheep, Iran
Bruce Davidson/Magnum

Nail shoes at Kumbh Mela festival, India
Baldev/Sygma

Sandals with orange pom poms, Ivory Coast
Betty Press/Woodfin Camp

Native American shoes, USA
J. Pat Carter/Liaison Agency

Orange rollerskates, USA
Levy/Liaison Agency

Man with bundles of plastic sandals, Mali
Ian Berry/Magnum

POW wearing makeshift shoes, Iraq/Turkey border
Patrick Robert/Sygma Press

Swanky snowboots, Switzerland
Toni Anzenberger/ Anzenberger

Impoverished children sharing one pair of shoes, Nigeria
Ian Berry/Magnum

Witch doctor in costume, Lesotho
Chris Steel-Perkins /Magnum

Sandals worn to symbolize horse hoofs, India
Gelles Mermet/ Liaison Agency

WORK

Two chimney sweeps, France
Elliott Erwitt/Magnum

Man in shirt, tie, and skirt, Western Samoa
Dilip Mehta/Contact Press

Farm worker, South Africa
Alon Reininger/Contact

Solderers at oil rig, Nigeria
Abbas/Magnum

Rex Hotel bellhops, Vietnam
Alain Evrard/Liaison Agency

Couple with goose, Latvia
Tass/Sovfoto/Eastfoto

Cocktail hostesses, France
Bruno Bebert/Sipa Press

Plaza Athenee Hotel waiter, France
Rene Burri/Magnum

Fisherman, Portugal
Bruno Barbey/Magnum

Kitchen workers, Ukraine
Bruno Barbey/Magnum

Sugar cane cutters, Cuba
Abbas/Magnum

Man carrying a very
big paiche fish to the
market, Peru
Alex Webb/Magnum

PLAY

Cricketeer, Jamaica
Dennis Stock/Magnum

Women in exercise
class, Cuba
Alex Webb/Magnum

Stag hunt, France
Bruno Barbey/Magnum

Sumo wrestlers, Hawaii, USA
Robb Kendrick/Aurora

HUMAN STORES

Woman with sewing machine
on head, Zaire
Jose Azel/Contact Press

Woman with chard
on head, Spain
Stuart Franklin/Magnum

Woman with milk cartons on
head, South Africa
Alon Reininger/Contact Press

Woman carrying bananas
on head, Ghana
Ian Berry/Magnum

Woman carrying newspapers
on head, South Korea
Ron Levy/Liaison Agency

Women with towels on head,
Lome Grande Marche, Africa
Wendy Stone/Liaison Agency

Woman with platters
on head, Iraq
Abbas/Magnum

Women with containers on
heads, South Africa
Alon Reininger/Contact Press

Children with buckets on
heads, South Africa
Alon Reininger/Contact Press

EXTREME CONDITIONS

Dr. J. L. Etiennie on foot to
the North Pole, Arctic Circle
E. Preau/Sygma

Warfare training for the
Red Army, Russia
Hans J. Burkhard/Aurora

Radiation testers in white,
five years after Chernobyl,
Russia
Tass/Sovfoto

Fireman from chemical fire
division in Moscow, Russia
J. B. Diederich/Contact Press

Fire-fighting monks of
Niepokalanow, Poland
*W. P. Rey Germain/
Liaison Agency*

French students in net helmets
Erik Sampers/Liaison Agency

Sanitation specialists, Zaire
Stuart Franklin/Magnum

Three boys near factory, India
J.P. Laffont/Sygma

Steel mill worker, South Africa
Alon Reininger/Contact Press

Policeman in futuristic
protective gear, UK
*Grosset-Spooner/
Liaison Agency*

Scientist in red protective
gear, Artic Circle
E. Preau/Sygma

Inuit hunter in polar bear
skin, Greenland
*Bryan and Cherry Alexander/
Still Pictures*

VERY EXTREME CONDITIONS

Woman wearing garbage
bags, USA
*Andrew Holbrooke/
Liaison Agency*

Man on street, Guatemala
Chris Steele-Perkins/Magnum

SOLOS

Man walking down
street, Russia
*Gueorgui Pinkhassov/
Magnum*

Dervish, Turkey
Roland & Sabrina Michaud/
Woodfin Camp

The Corkman at Coney
Island's Mermaid Parade, USA
J. C. Bourcart/Liaison Agency

Man in suit, France
Bruno Barbey/Magnum

Masai Mara woman in
doorway, Kenya
Betty Press/Woodfin Camp

Girl wrapped in red
coat, Spain
David Alan Harvey/Magnum

Man in costume at Corpus
Christi festival, Peru
Robert Frerck/Woodfin Camp

Woman in black with basket
of flowers, Portugal
Bruno Barbey/Magnum

Tibetan woman with prayer
beads, Nepal
Steve McCurry/Magnum

Commercial fisherman, USA
Peter Essick/Aurora

Medicine man, Africa
Wendy Watriss/
Woodfin Camp

Woman clasping chains, Iran
Eric Brissaud/Liaison Agency

Girl in white, Russia
Lise Sarfati/Magnum

Woman in kimono, Japan
Yuen Lee/Liaison Agency

Cloaked man at Semana
Santa festival, Spain
Jonathan Elderfield/
Liaison Agency

Desert patrolman, Jordan
Brian Smith/Liaison Agency

Tribal woman with pipe, China
Eve Arnold/Magnum

Woman in blue, Brazil
Abbas/Magnum

Boy with box on head,
Anguilla
Maira Kalman

DUOS

Two men on Kumbh Mela
pilgrimage, India
Giboux/Liaison Agency

Two women at East Hampton
at garden party, USA
Mark Peterson/Saba

Boys in matching suits,
Turkey
Roland & Sabrina Michaud/
Woodfin Camp

Two men in sarongs, India
Sarah Caron/Liaison Agency

Newlyweds. Groom is
seven years old and the
bride is five, India
Raghu Rai/Magnum

Bahau couple, Borneo
Kal Muller/Woodfin Camp

Two smiling men, South Africa
Alon Reininger/Contact Press

Father and son at James
Bond festival, Jamaica
Martin Parr/Magnum

HOLYWEAR

Cloak worn by St. Francis
of Assisi, Italy
Maira Kalman collection

Australian monk in sensible
shoes, Egypt
Abbas/Magnum

Mevlevi dervishes, Turkey
Adam Woolfitt/Woodfin Camp

Catholic priests, Vatican City
Giansanti/Sygma

Jimmy Swaggart at Nassau
Coliseum, NY
Steve McCurry/Magnum

Buddhist monks, Burma
Geoffrey Hiller

French Nun in prayer, Bosnia
N. Econompoulos/Magnum

Muslim men praying, Malaysia
Abbas/Magnum

Italian bishops, Vatican City
Giansanti/Sygma

The Nagas or The Naked
Renouncers, India
Giboux/Liaison Agency

Woman at Holy Festival, Iran
Abbas/Magnum

Woman in black mantilla
during Holy Week, Spain
F. Scianna/Magnum

Orthodox Jews in
Yeshiva, Israel
Patrick Zachman/Magnum

Boy wearing cross, Sudan
*Alexandra Avakian/
Contact Press*

Face of Jesus painted on
African boubou, France
Abbas/Magnum Photos

DEATH

Infant in coffin, Brazil
Abbas/Magnum

Funeral dress parlor, China
Xinhua/Liaison Agency

Mother of Disappeared
keeps vigil, Mexico
Abbas/Magnum

Funeral procession,
Guatemala
Gilles Peress/Magnum

Funerary pajamas, Hong Kong
Davies + Starr

Funerary pajamas, Hong Kong
Davies + Starr

Gule Wam Kulu dancer
dressed for funeral, Malawi
Eli Reed/Magnum

Woman in white wailing,
Vietnam
Larry Towell/Magnum

Family sitting with
deceased, Nigeria
Bruno Barbey/Magnum

Family members around
deceased at Buddhist
funeral, Sri Lanka
Bruno Barbey/Magnum

Palanquin with body of
Emperor Hirohito, carried by
51 Shinto priests, Japan
P. J. Griffith/Magnum

The body of Lebanese major
Saad Haddad being carried
to village community center,
Lebanon
Michar Baram/Magnum

(re)Birth

Baby bundle on carpet,
Armenia
Armineh Johannes/Sipa

CHEERS

Nuba man, Sudan
*Peter Moszynski/
Panos Pictures*

Editor: Ruth A. Peltason

Copyright © 2000
Maira Kalman

ISBN 1-86154-144-9

Published in all territories outside
USA by Booth-Clibborn Editions

(un)FASHION *was created and
designed by M&Co, New York*

**TIBOR + MAIRA
KALMAN**
Creative Directors

KEVIN KWAN
Photo Editor

LARA HARRIS
Designer

THANK YOU
Dena Bunge
Ben Kombol
Meaghan Kombol
Nico Muhly
Jessica Murray
Ruth A. Peltason
Pete
Charlotte Sheedy
The amazing photographers
  participating in this book
And dear Chalkie Davies

Printed and bound
in Hong Kong

Booth Clibborn Editions
12 Percy Street
London W1P 9FB
www.booth-clibborn.com
info@booth-clibborn.com

CHEERS